Redditch

on old picture postcard

CW00742637

Volume 2

Chris Jackson

1. Evesham Street at its junction with George Street. The "Hungry Man" public house is on the right and will be remembered by many for its revolving door. Evesham Street Post Office is on the left and the narrow opening on the left is Littleworth. Card sent from Redditch to Weston-super-Mare on 2nd May 1952.

£3.50

2. A composite card from the 1960s with St. Stephen's in the centre, Market Place with Woolworth's top left, Alcester Street with the "Palace Theatre" in the distance top right, The Parade (Church Green West) is bottom left and the Green with the fountain bottom right.

Designed and Published by
Reflections of a Bygone Age,
Keyworth, Nottingham
1995

ISBN 1 900138 01 8

Printed by
Adlard Print and Typesetting Services,
Ruddington, Notts.

3. The Institute in Church Road, built in 1886 at a cost of £2,700. When this card was posted in August 1905, the Institute contained over 3000 volumes and had over 250 members. Visitors could get admission to the reading room on payment of one penny. The building now contains the college training restaurant. Postcard published by Valentine of Dundee.

4. Photographic card of 'The Parade' with a Midland Red bus waiting to leave for Studley, and another in the layby at the end of William Street. The drinking fountain is on the left and there is no sign of the traffic lights which were a feature of the junction for many years. Card posted to Hereford on 24th August 1931.

INTRODUCTION

Anyone who has seen my first book on Redditch will already know that I am Redditch born and bred and that my collection of postcards stems originally from a keen interest in philately.

When my first book was about to be published I was quite apprehensive. I wondered if it would succeed in bringing back memories of the town for the people who had lived in Redditch and give newer inhabitants an idea of how the town used to be.

Judging by the many comments and telephone calls I received, the book certainly achieved the first objective, and I am grateful to everyone who made contact, some with more information and some just to talk through old times.

Probably the most common question has been *"When will the next book be published?"* Well here it is! I hope you get as much enjoyment from it as I have had preparing it.

Picture Postcards were first published in Britain in 1894, but it was not until a decade later that they began to take off, when in 1902 the Post Office allowed a message to be written on the address side. This meant that the whole of one side was available for the picture and obviously gave more scope to publishers. Photographic viewcards became very popular, and the postcard became the most important way of communicating news or messages, in much the same way as the telephone is used today. The years up to 1914 were the 'Golden Age' of picture postcards, when millions of imaginative designs covering every subject under the sun were published by a host of national and local firms. There's hardly a village or hamlet that wasn't documented at that time by a postcard publisher, though sometimes the number of cards available was unrelated to the size of a community.

There are a selection of cards from the main publishers in the area: A Harold Clarke, L.L. Sealey, A. Green, F.A. Hodges, Joe Harman and Lewis Bros. The age of the cards varies from 1902 up to the 1960's. Postcards by national publishers like Valentine of Dundee and W.H. Smith are also featured in this volume.

Some cards are cross-referenced to pictures in the first book.

I have attempted to ensure the details contained in this book are correct. If I have made a mistake please forgive me, but let me know! I am always interested in obtaining more detailed information and expanding my collection. I can be contacted on (01527) 544722.

Chris Jackson
November 1995

Front cover: A super photographic card published by A. Green of the market on Market Place in the 1920s showing many contrasting style of dress. The market existed along the church railings for many years and many of the older inhabitants can remember it.

18—34   SMALLWOOD HOSPITAL, REDDITCH

5. The Smallwood Hospital at the top of Prospect Hill, built by the Smallwood Brothers and opened in May 1895. The trees were a feature of the Parade for many years and were regularly pruned back heavily as in this card, published by E.A. Hodges of Redditch in the 1930s.

6. The rear of the Smallwood Hospital on a card sent from Redditch to Sheffield on 16th October 1909. This is a view of the hospital that is not nearly as common as the front of the building and which was taken before the extension was added.

7. St. Stephen's Church viewed from William Street on a photographic card sent from Redditch to Derby in July 1925.

8. The Northern end of Church Green with the Bandstand and the Fountain in a separate area. The road on the left was Church Avenue, later to be pedestrianised and the site of a pair of telephone boxes. Card used on 23rd June 1906 to wish *'Happy Birthday'* to Mrs. Bell, Music W'House, Redditch.

9. Late 1930's card by Valentine of Dundee of Church Green East and Church Green with a 'Belisha' crossing across Church Green East at its junction with Easemore Road.

135/3 The Fountain, Church Green, Redditch

10. The Fountain on Church Green. It was given to the town by the Bartleet family in 1883 when mains water was brought to the town. The building on the left at the end of the Green was the public toilet, which was removed when the underground toilets on Church Green West were built. Card posted to Yeadon in May 1936.

11. Published by L.L. Sealey of Beoley Road, Redditch, this postcard shows the top of Prospect Hill with Hills Yard on the left and the "Crown Hotel" in the centre of the picture. Edward Perks offered '*Holders Ales, Choice Wines and Spirits, Bowling Green, Billiards and Stabling*'. The ringway now crosses Prospect Hill just below the Crown. Card sent to Worcester in May 1911.

12. A Raphael Tuck card (c.1958) of Prospect Hill showing Clarkes "Sinew" Works, which occupied the hill from the vicarage to the doctor's surgery. Besides the car (registration KOB 121) on the left, the Co-op bread van and a Midland Red bus are clearly visible going down the hill.

13. Birmingham Road at its junction with Clive Road at the bottom of Prospect Hill. The houses on the right are little changed and the gap in the houses became the entrance to the Abbey Hostel, now Fishing Line road. The gate on the left was to Brunswick House where the Bennett family lived.

14. The "Toll House" which stood at the junction with Dagnell End Road and the A441 Birmingham Road, opposite Bordesley Garage. It was the home of Granny Locke, and had a central living room with bedrooms either side and a kitchen at the rear. Unfortunately, when it became derelict it was demolished instead of being moved to Avoncroft.

CHURCH GREEN EAST, REDDITCH.

15. A 1902 card of Church Green East. Until the Post Office Act of 1902, cards could only have the address on the reverse, and any message had to be on the same side as the picture. Card sent from Redditch to Scarborough on 5th January 1903.

RD 2   ALCESTER STREET, REDDITCH   A TUCK CARD

16. A 1950's Tuck card of Alcester Street from its junction with Church Green East and Market Place. Murdoch's outfitters is next door to Dyers ("your ironmonger") and further down the street is Palmer's Corn Stores, Hedges Chemist and Popham's, "The Baby Shop". The "Regent" sign on the right was Regent Motorways, adjacent to Fairest's toy shop.

17. Alcester Street on a W.H. Smith 'Kingsway' series card posted to London on 12th July 1913. Walter Smith's grocery shop is on the right and the huge advert for Milward's on the corner of Grove Street proclaims *'Church & House Painters, Signwriters, Grainers and Gilders'*. On the left, Alfred Lewis offers umbrella repairs and 'The Acme Toilet Club'!

18. Photographic card of Beoley Road, posted to Headingley on 1st November 1912, written by M.E. Smith from the Post Office next door to the "Cricketers Arms". The archway led through to 'Neptune Works', a needle, fish hook and leather factory. The "Cricketers Arms" is much the same today, except it has lost its ornate light.

19. The entrance to Evesham Street, with a policeman controlling the traffic, Huins, Hodges and Boots the Chemist (with an enormous sign) are on the left and Cranmore Simmons is behind the tree on the right. A Valentine postcard c.1937.

20. A Hodges card of Evesham Street c.1913 taken from the top of Worcester Road looking towards Church Green. Liptons is on the corner of New Street. Later it became Hopkins the jewellers. The "Maypole" occupied the opposite corner of New Street. The "Vine Inn" is on the left, later rebuilt as the "Talbot".

21. Marvellous animation on this Edwardian street scene. A Clarke's card of Evesham Street full of people and activity. Gray's Tobacconist is on the left (it later became Preedy's). Brough's outfitters and Field's confectioners and cafe were along the street.

Clarkes. 16A.

On the right is Guise's Silversmiths and Watchmaker, with a clock above the doorway. Note the lady cyclist! Card posted on 6th July 1907.

22. A card of Evesham Street sent to France on 8th July 1922 showing T. Haines & Sons (outfitters) and Home & Colonial, the grocers, on the left. On the left is Worcester Road, which went past the Temperance Hall and down a steep hill to the Railway Station.

23. The Congregational Church built by Thomas Williams, a needlemaker, adjacent to his house and factory in Evesham Street. The graveyard in front of the church became known as the "Needlemakers Graveyard" due to the number buried there. It is now approximately the site of Mothercare in the Kingfisher Shopping Centre.

24. The "Unicorn" Public House at the top of Unicorn Hill about 1906. 'Mr. Ricketts, Grocer and Tea Dealer', is far more prominent than the pub itself. The hanging sign and the ornate railings with the lamp over the steps were particularly fine.

25. The top of Unicorn Hill at the junction with Bates Hill. The house on the right is now a locksmiths, and the house in the centre is Hemmings, estate agents. The two houses on the left were demolished to build the cinema.

S 3892

MIDLAND RAILWAY

26. Redditch Railway Station when it was a Midland sta
bridge was a footbridge over the tracks and Bromsgrove F
on 8th August 1911, and published by W.H. Smith Ltd.

ATION, REDDITCH.

with an engine approaching the platform. The latticework
bridge is behind. Card posted from Salford Priors to France

27. St. Benedict's Cottage, off Stevenson Avenue at the back of Mount Carmel Church. The card was posted to London on 20th December 1920 and the writer Agnes Wilson refers to *"having the wish of my life – a little house close to the church in a place where there is no society but plenty of work to be done for the church"*.

28. The Police Station in Church Road with the Court House next door on a card posted from Redditch on 19th May 1911 to Hanbury. The buildings were demolished to make way for Car Park Seven and the new Adelaide Street.

Redditch.   The Post Office.

29. The Post Office, which was in Church Road for many years. The sorting office was behind, together with the telegram office. The Telephone Exchange was built next door between the Post Office and the Police Station. The building still exists and is now the County Court.

30. Ipsley Street just below its junction with Millsboro Road. The shop that was Mrs. Jarvis's sweet shop still exists and is now a travel agents. Millwards factory *(see illus. 44, volume 1)*, was behind the railings on the left. The "Kings Arms" and Mount Carmel church are in the distance. Card posted to Cheltenham in May 1921.

Ipsley St Redditch

31. The Woodland Cottage on Mount Pleasant when it had a front garden. The driver of the car appears to be oblivious to the motorcycle and sidecar coming up Mount Pleasant. The writer says she *"arrived home at 8.10 p.m. (12th Aug. 1924) in the middle of a thunderstorm"*.

32. Mount Pleasant at Headless Cross in the 1920s. The houses on the left are little changed, and the house on the right is now a nursing home. The paved area was the entrance to the Terry's house which is now the "Southcrest Hotel".

33. A card published by R.A.P. & Co. in the 1930's of the main road junction at Headless Cross, where the A448 Birchfield Road from Bromsgrove met the A441 Birmingham to Evesham Road. The shop on the left became Miss Gardner's. Bird's (butchers) on the corner of Highfield Road became the Midland Bank and is now "The Flower Lady".

34. The "Fleece Hotel" at Crabbs Cross at the junction of Littelwoods and the Evesham Road. Card sent from Barmouth to Liverpool on 7th November 1905. The message from Charlie says *"the centre one of the three in the doorway is yours truly."*

ENFIELD FACTORY HUNT END .2.

35. A photographic card of the Enfield Factory on Enfield Road at Hunt End. The picture was taken before the houses were built on the east side of the road and clearly shows how extensive the factory was. Card postally used from Redditch to Gloucester on 14th May 1907; the writer gives his address as "Airlie Cottage", Crabbs Cross, off the map!

RECTORY RD. HEADLESS CROSS.

EDKINS' SERIES

36. Wyatt's Garage nearing completion at the junction of Rectory and Plymouth Roads at Nailpasser Green, Headless Cross. Note the Shell pumps with the long arms to extend to the offside of vehicles. The premises are now a tyre company. Card published in the 'Edkins' series.

37. Birchfield Road with two horses and carts and only one car in the distance. The houses on the left are little changed today and until recently the road would have been much busier. Now it is no longer a through road for vehicles it may have reverted to the peaceful road it appears here.

P.O..SERIES.   HILL TOP. WEB HEATH.

38. Hill Top at Webheath on a 1920's card sent to Abbotts Bromley wishing Miss Greaves best wishes with her exams. The house in the centre still exists but those to the right have been replaced with an estate which stretches across the fields. Note the man in the road: he appears to be collecting something in a bucket; for his rhubarb, perhaps?

REDDITCH

39. A photographic card taken from the top of St. Stephens spire in 1905 *(see illus. 21, volume 1)*. It is the view to the west of the church down William Street to Adelaide Street and the railway sidings beyond. The large building left of centre is Bates Hill Methodist Church, and beyond that is a footbridge over the railway.

40. Heathfield Road, Webheath, on a 'P.O. Series' card. The horse-drawn bread wagon was owned by Mr. Bonaker, who had his bakery on Birchfield Road. The message on the card says *"I got the knickers safely – they fit nicely now"!*

41. A composite card of Astwood Bank published by C. Hodges, and sent to Kings Heath in July 1916. Doe Bank House is in the centre and Evesham Road is top left; the drive (to Doe Bank House) is top right, Astwood Lane is bottom left and Chapel Street bottom right.

42. The Evesham Road at its junction with Avenue Road, with the building on the corner is the "Bell Inn". The house next door has an ornate light proclaiming it as the "Woodman Inn". Card posted from Astwood Bank to Bromsgrove on 17th January 1908.

43. A photographic card of the enlargement of St. Matthias and St. George Church at Astwood Bank. The work was carried out by Huxleys, a local company whose hut is in the background. The vicar is at the centre watching the photographer, as are all the workmen. Card sent to Bromyard on 20th May 1911.

44. Evesham Road, Astwood Bank, at its junction with Feckenham Road and Sambourne Lane looking south. The houses and the "White Lion" are much the same today as they were when this card was posted to Rugby on 29th November 1906. A recent addition to the junction is a set of traffic lights.

45. A Clarke's (Windsor Portrait Galleries of Redditch) card of the corner of Easemore and Other Roads. The writer has written on the face of the card to identify their house. It was sent from Redditch to Pennsylvania, USA, on 7th February 1914 and the message refers to the writer's delight at having *"12 rooms, a bathroom and electric light"*. Presumably America was a bit behind us then!

46. Easemore Road, looking east towards Beoley Church. The picture was taken from outside the entrance to what is now the Abbey High School.

47. Archer Road on a photographic card of c.1908. The houses are unchanged. The railings on the right were to St. Stephens school *(see illus. 34, volume 1),* now the N.E.W. college.

RDH.35. THE LAKES, BATCHLEY ESTATE. REDDITCH.

48. The lakes at Batchley on a Frith card sent from Redditch to Holland on 7th July 1966. The building on the extreme right is part of Bridley Moor High School.

WEBB & SONS

49. Church Green East in the 1950's with Webb & Sons' bakery on the corner of Peakman Street. The upper storeys are unchanged, but the shopfronts are very different. Compare this view to the one in illus. 9 of volume 1.

50. The vicarage built for the vicar of St. Stephens, situated behind the houses on Plymouth Road and Vicarage View but accessed from Bromsgrove Road. It has now been demolished to make way for the houses on Prophets Close. Card posted to Atherstone in August 1913.

51. A 'Clarke's Series' card of 'Muskatts Way', sent from Redditch to Sparkhill on 22nd September 1906. The path which joins Birchfield Road with Bromsgrove Road still exists. It now goes over a high bridge spanning the Bromsgrove Highway, leading past the golf course and through to Vicarage Crescent and Bromsgrove Road.

52. A posed card of W.F. Tayler, baker and confectioner, dating from c.1920. Mr. Tayler's bakehouse was in Beaufort Street behind what is now Baker's the butcher!

53. One of a long series of cards (this is number 12) depicting the Eadie Sports days. This one shows the start of the 6th heat of the 300 yards race held on 21st July 1906. There must have been plenty of competitors to have needed so many heats!

54. Sid Green's hairdressing shop which was at the top of Beoley Road, with Sid in the doorway. Notice the striped barber's pole and that in addition to haircuts he offered *'Shaving, Singeing & Shampooing'*. Card sent from Redditch to Scarborough on 24th August 1925.

55. The marchers in this Labour demonstration on 27th July 1907 are coming down Evesham Street to Church Green. Notice the hats: everyone is wearing one of some sort – cap, boater or bowler for the men and a variety of fancy bonnets for the ladies. The card was sent to Alcester on 30th July from New Street and asks the receiver to *"find Marjorie and me in the picture"*.

THE GARDEN OF REMEMBRANCE, REDDITCH.

56. The entrance to the Garden of Remembrance on Plymouth Road on a card published by H. Wilkes, Railway Approach, Redditch. The cemetery is in the background and the sign inside the gate is by the "Joint Burial Committee". Bentley Close is opposite this entrance.

Memorial, Garden of Remembrance, Redditch

57. The War Memorial in the Gardens of Remembrance. The inscription refers to *"those of Redditch who in the Great War faced death for freedom and passed out of our sight"* and in reference to the Second World War *"those of this town who gave their lives when Freedom was again in danger 1939/45"*. Card published by E.A. Hodges.